The National Poetry Series

The National Poetry Series was established in 1978 to publish five collections of poetry annually through five participating publishers. The manuscripts are selected by five poets of national reputation. Publication is funded by James A. Michener, Edward J. Piszek, The Ford Foundation, The Witter Bynner Foundation, and the five publishers—Doubleday, E. P. Dutton, Harper & Row, Random House, and Holt, Rinehart and Winston.

THE NATIONAL POETRY SERIES — 1980

Sterling A. Brown, *Collected Poems* (Selected by Michael Harper)

Joseph Langland, *Any Body's Song* (Selected by Ann Stanford)

Ronald Perry, *Denizens* (Selected by Donald Justice)

Wendy Salinger, *Folly River* (Selected by Donald Hall)

Roberta Spear, *Silks* (Selected by Philip Levine)

SILKS

SILKS

POEMS BY **Roberta Spear**

HOLT, RINEHART AND WINSTON   NEW YORK

Published by Holt, Rinehart and Winston,
383 Madison Avenue, New York, New York 10017.
Published simultaneously in Canada by
Holt, Rinehart and Winston of Canada, Limited.

Library of Congress Cataloging in Publication Data
Spear, Roberta.
Silks.
I. Title.
PS3569.P395S5   811'.5'4   79-19210
ISBN Hardbound: 0-03-056117-5
ISBN Paperback: 0-03-056116-7

First Edition
Designer: Joy Chu
Printed in the United States of America
10 9 8 7 6 5 4 3 2 1

I would like to thank the editors of the following
publications in which some of the poems
originally appeared:

Antaeus: "A Sale of Smoke," "The Bat"; Field:
"Rumor," "Terremoto: Antigua, 1976"; Ironwood:
"The Festival of Fatima," "Crows"; The Nation: "The
Anniversary"; The New Yorker: "The White Dress";
Quarterly West: "Eclipse," "Building a Small House";
Raccoon: "All Around Us"; The Seneca Review:
"Nightfall on Pacheco," "The Trees Began to Speak,"
"Eclipse," "Building a Small House," "The Fear of
Angels" (as "The Lust of Clouds"), "The Fiddler's
Wife," "Silks"; Westigan Review: "In Your Absence,"
"Story"; Valley Light: "The Healer," "The Traveler,"
"Story," "Tonsils," "Considering Fire"; The American
Poetry Anthology: "The Bat," "August/Fresno 1973,"
"A Sale of Smoke"; The Missouri Review: "Dust."

FOR BEERB AND MARION

Contents

ONE

BUILDING A
SMALL HOUSE

In the dream that pulls
me to the wall, a chill
rises from the mortar.
I watch carpenters perched
over the bare frame,
insects sailing
between the studs. An old man
carrying a bucket of plaster
moves toward me;
another measures
doorways wide enough
for diesels and clouds.

I can't understand
how these men keep
themselves in my dream.
I refuse to be the nail
that holds this place together.

*

In the old books
the carpenter shows up
before dawn, breaking
bread in his favor
with a silent partner.
The two watch women
dump garbage from the windows
and know that each village

has a genius who dies in bed,
but are never asked
for an opinion.
At the end of the day
they wipe their hands
on their undershirts
and vanish,
like air between the pages.

*

When I wake
there is a vein
of light on the shade.
They have left me
a soft foundation
under sheets imprinted
by children's hands,
and you who still hang high
in sleep, like a crane,
and can build
without lifting a finger.

Our imperfections
show up now—blotches
like rusty nails,
knots bored in sleep.
The earth shifts
inside of me:

When I was young
my father raised walls
of steam in the bathroom

and walked through them,
but came back each night
to disappear again.

*

Later the alley will rumble,
flies storm the trash.
The hammering begins.

Tract of lids, waxed peel
carved by blunt teeth,
shingle of fur—what I make
will be nameless.
A neighbor watches the apron
bulging at my waist
and spreads her sheets
on the line between us.
At dusk, her son will be
waiting in the shadows
to help me carry the tools.

ECLIPSE

We go out on the porch to watch
and already others are stretched out
on the grass or are leaning
on the hoods of dark cars.
The last glint is on earth:
a young man cups the lighted butt
to his mouth without looking down.

This makes me feel young again—
in all these years nothing I've learned
can shed light like this.

*

When they held me up to the basin
and dabbed my cheeks, I backed away
from the umbra of vestments,
from the father (not mine) who mouthed O
over and over, his eyes
on the water and the water no deeper
than a bowl of soup.

*

Everything changes:

the old priest dies,
the child is renamed,
the goat shaved until its belly
curves under like a pale melon
or the bow of a star-dazed ship.

We bathe ourselves for a world
that comes.

*

She pulls herself onto the bank
and wipes off the mud, her calves
glowing in the silver light.
She drives men mad with this
simple motion. Across the street
the young man puts his arm
around his woman, drunk
on the sway of gravity,
on the certainty of how far
he can go.

AUGUST/FRESNO 1973

Even the sun, still warm
and husky, seems silly
as it searches the alley
for some loose fur. This is why
I take my time.
I pull the curtains when I wake
and stand naked in front of the cooler.
I don't try to fool myself:
it takes three seconds
to fill an ice tray, two hours
to make cubes, forty minutes
for the ice to melt and form
a lake that fruit flies skid across
when I leave the room.
Somewhere in this town
I have a perfect mate: not the one
who fucks to forget the heat,
but a young man
who patiently places a match
between each toe for every blonde
that has left him.

THE FIDDLER'S WIFE

Late at night
my husband plays the fiddle
by a candle in his study.
His eyes are heavy
and he is always learning.
Pumping has thickened his right arm
as autumn has the evening air
with its blendings of smoke
and color, and nothing
interrupts him—

not the copper chimes
turned by the wind,
nor the sound of his own heart.

Shadows steal the spindled notes
before they reach me in my sleep
many rooms away,
and what I finally hear is darkness

breaking in my body,
a fine tune.

*

I can't decide if its rosy flanks
remind me of a man's or a woman's.
Those who've shouldered this angel
through a gallant reel
have lived in neither world:

the blind fiddler who feels the breeze
of a woman's skirt, the one with a nose so big
he must cock his head to the right
to receive his own music, the drunkard
surviving below all vibrations.

These though are the masters.
Their secrets are the rosin
drained from the oldest trees,
a loneliness that undresses itself
again and again.

*

You tell me the story of Stradivari
who must have left his own wife before dawn
to pace the empty docks
as the bow of a merchant ship
was dredged from the pale water.

You explain the mystery of mahogany
cured in brine,
urchin-stained, the pitch
of oxygen trapped in this perfect wood.

If Antonio got his bargain
in the mellow curve and vibrato
of a flowering world, he also
loaded his heart onto this vessel
that now carries you away.

At sunrise
he returned to his bed,

remembering the delicate slits,
the dark veneer of a mouth
that never closes . . .

*

I should have known when I married
a man who plays the fiddle . . .

In the shadows
I can see the shape of my hand.
Its fingers, too small and uncalloused,
mean nothing at my own task.

I should have known on that first night,
in the kitchen
lit by a single bulb,
when the music of seven men
ran the color of whiskey
and I learned that the finest strings
come from the guts of a cat.

But what could I say
when I only knew how to sing it,
the high wail of Appalachia
caught in the back of the throat,
as we left the house
for the cool air of the country
where it all began,
arm in arm,
the eyes of stars on us.

IN YOUR ABSENCE
FOR JEFF

In uneven gasps the sewing machine
takes from my fingers
the starched edge of a sleeve.
The cogs' bullheaded spinning
tells me I don't have
my mother's touch.
After two months,
it is always this way,
everything fights back:
the cat drinks from the toilet,
the neighbor boy revs his Chevy
as he passes our house,
my sex dreams fill me,
so many green apples.

When you come home
at the end of the week
it will be foggy here
and my face will be blurred.
Don't look for the changes.
When I yell at you, listen
to the love poem. The windowpanes
have warmed in your absence.
And if my fingers cramp
it's because they've made
a shirt that can be worn now,
with a patch that's been sewn
many times.

THE HEALER

1

The dust trembles,
the pale splintered benches
are lined up under the tent.
When the preacher stretches
his fingers in midair,
the people rise,
bowing to the Word.
A woman's tongue straightens,
a child faints,
a real believer promises
to run up through that ring
of fog on the slender crests
of the Ozarks.

2

When I was a child
old Omeda would tell us
to "dounce the glim"
and sent us to bed
with warm poultices—
good dreams were the cure
for everything.
But we passed messages
across the dark river
or threw shadows onto the wall
with our small white fingers
while she cried herself to sleep.

3

It is almost dark:
the crepe myrtle
hangs to the ground,
like feathery jowls,
and a faithful breeze lifts
the old blossoms off the grass,
rearranging them in air.

I want you to follow
me out and feel it
for yourself—the way
the fog places a hand
on your head.
But you stand at the mirror,
pulling a new blade
down your cheek, swearing
as the last hairs swirl
down the drain.

THE ANNIVERSARY

It's the first of May—
the last drops of rain are a payment
to the dust and yellow air.
The man beside me preserves dreams
in his dark folds. When the light
settles on the walls, he turns
restlessly as a saint
whose limbs are buried in different cities.
I loosen the fist of sheets,
the clouds move on and return.
After each breath,
he breathes again.

Hours ago, we drove back to town,
the sky contracted on all sides
bolting the branches along the road.
We drank to years of labor,
the ladder of love, to the corn
illumined, growing up into the dead
of night, the vineyards
glowing like spines.
We passed a woman outside a country bar;
under the awning with a cigarette,
she gave quickly to the streams
of alkali, small rivers
filling the furrows.

The possibilities are as endless
as watermarks in the dust.

But in town, it's only rain
and is gone. The first yeses sprout
in a patch of purple outside the window,
an elm bows over the universe
of our bed. Only the two of us,
and you're gone, staggering
into sleep like that senseless jay
through loops of gravel and wet leaves
to his home in the air.
It is as clear as vodka:

I want to wake you now,
saying let's drink up and get back
to the work we did so well last night,
saying as the earth says after rain
this one is on me.

BOUNDARIES

I clipped and the brown petals
piled on the driveway.
Two neighbors marked boundaries
set thirty years ago.
There were certain things
they couldn't say to each other:
One brushed the dirt off
on her washdress and the other
blamed a man who came to the house
when she was a child.

Later, I fought with myself
while trying to plant
a row of seeds on the edge
of this paper. I left the desk
for a pair of socks
and a cigarette. I thought
of my sister's wedding, of days
when we were told that nothing
was too good for us.

        My father
under the arbor
of dried concords, filled
his glass over and over;
my grandmother moved her chair
into the sun and settled;
I froze under the bridesmaid's ruffle,
neither fainting nor feeling

the blood in my cheeks.
At dusk, the cyclamen stiffened
on the covered tables.

Yet, if my sister asked,
I would tell her that boundaries
mean nothing. I have a husband
and we come together
in the afternoon. She and I
came together too,
were overheard
and put into separate rooms.

As I clipped, their voices
flew off with robins.
And my eyes followed
a bud in the shadows
kissing its way
into this world.

THE WHITE DRESS

I want you to see me in it.

The mirror witches an image
that invents every movement. When I spin
I enter the seven precious stages of flight;
the room is as lively as a dovecote.
Again I turn and stop,
looking into your eyes
where the feathers are drifting down
over my thighs and knees.
The cloth obeys the curves of my body.
It is as simple as this,
a white dress.

Later we will leave the party and walk
the cool sidewalks toward the highway
where junipers nod in the wind.
When my skirt ripples out into darkness
you will move me, like a sail
in its first gentle breaths
toward the open sea. White
is a mixture of many understandings.

The bare arm,
the angle of fiber on skin,
two thin strings at the neck
undoing the world . . .
Now turn away.

Sunlight is living in the storefront window
and the shopkeeper wants her money.
I want your opinion

years from now
when you've forgotten how I look in white.

IF I CAN'T SLEEP

If I can't sleep
it's because they are dancing,
black pines that grew too fast.
The moon has its hands full:
they dip and curtsy
or shoot straight up
above their sullen shadows.
I too follow the warm passages,
coming as close to you as possible.
This is how we learned to dance.

Left arm around the neck,
right arm on the chest,
breast and thigh poured slowly
into one cup that never filled.
He gathered me from the row
of metal chairs, my face scarred
and blackened as the drum skin
by each beat and violet strobe.
Afterward, the girls went back
to the bathroom to study themselves
for hidden signs or lucky ones.
But we were not allowed
to look at the moon
that held us as we grew.

Making rounds in the pasture of stars,
the moon turns serious
and leans toward me,

blowing his final smoke in my eyes.
Unable to speak his mind,
he spies on me like this,
in bed with my man;
I turn away to the wall
of sleep. There, another horizon:

a thin blue line
that winds away from the dancers,
a thread that sews memories
to dreams, or snags
in a zipper half down.

CONSIDERING FIRE

I try to name
the last noises,
the possibilities of danger
while I sleep:
the asthmatic singing
of our neighbor's girl,
summer wind sugaring
the dry leaves, cars a mile off
down the main road,
a man's empty clothes.

As a child
I dreamed that fire would send me
out into the damp grass,
the singed curtains drifting
through the windows—
into morning, the cotton tatters
hooked in the upper branches
of mulberries along the block.
But this new house is cement:
the paint smudges,
the nails give.
Once the laboratory of a doctor,
our bedroom is the recovery room
where the floors drain—
it is so sound
that nothing happens.

Throwing shadows
across my legs, the sheet

unrolls like a list
of what to take or leave:
the person sleeping next to me,
too heavy to carry,
my cactus pregnant
in its tin pot,
the words of certain friends—
the little fires
that burn anywhere.

 TWO

FROM MEMORY

At night,
after we've turned away from each other,
my mind flowers wildly.
A magnolia opens under my eyelids,
like a cloud unfolding
or a baker pulling dough into two soft mounds.
I want to remember holding
this whiteness,
but the winds lift the petals,
the pale faces smoke into the real night;
the flames hiss and go out.
In the morning, I remember nothing.

And so it is, the sunlight stretches
over the walls and I enter
a shade of green no plant would ever be.
Its molded edges cling to shadows
where a gardener begs the roses to grow.
So it is, an old woman
follows me into the office with children
whose faces are sewn to her skirt.
The way I say "no" to them
lacks power—the sun swallowed,
the blossom unclenched.

Men come later in the day
with long faces, men
who, like me, forget who they are.
I offer them the vision

of a pale cheek as it turns to the sun,
the pencil that can be held
like a stamen
locked inside leaves.
I do forget,
though it will soon be night
and the eucalyptus yawns
and batters the window,
leaving a space that still fills with light.

THINGS MOST OFTEN
LEFT BEHIND

1

The easy lacework of the streetlight
and leaves on the blackened window—
a vision beautiful and frightening.
Our neighbor stands on his porch
staring out into the night,
preserving a secret he'll take
to his grave. His pipe smoke
drifts up through the telephone wires
to the moon that wears it
like a nightgown. He taps
the tiny bowl on his palm
and the dark flakes scatter,
the last seeds of a man.

2

To say he knows it will rain
would not be true; or that he sees
his own muddy tracks on the sidewalk
before daylight; to say he hears
the party of nameless birds
chattering under the wooden eaves
of his house in anticipation
would be foolish.
He simply needs something to cover him,
something less than the sky,
but more than the woman he's never had,

or closer to him than a house.
A shelter for someone just his size.
At the door, an umbrella is sleeping wisely—
will it open its wings
and be found again?

3

Then finally the rain falls
like teeth biting the earth;
and when he dies,
we stand over him grinning
unaware of how we look.
Teeth are the last thing to be forgotten,
because in the end food is soft
and the breath falters further down.
Even now, his shine through the hard layers
as he smiles back at us,
knowing his secret is well hidden.

DUST

FOR ELIZABETH COTTON

I know that it comes from the ground,
the jittery skin of hardpan.
But *oh* how the wind seems to own it,
making it rise and move through us
though we'd swear we'd seen nothing.

When I was a young woman
he took me to the cemetery on Saturdays
where we spread out
under a few toothless oaks
to stare down in silence at the valley
baking in the afternoon.
I smoothed my yellow skirt
into its own valleys
where he put his head and slept,
so happily. I still don't shudder
when I think of the dead.

See how it masks the faces of this valley,
how it makes the chard and bluegrass
rattle like ghosts.
See how one sparrow becomes two
that never age, how the eyes
wall up and the tongue thickens.
Folks have to take the train
to get back to where they belong.
I've run through dust
trying to reach the love in you
and found an early grave.

This is why I sing.
My voice is the fist of gravel
children fling at an old woman.
I pick up the broom,
beat the step, and laugh at dust
so they'll know I'm still alive.

ALL AROUND US

In a battered house,
on a street named after George Washington,
he is waiting to die.
Mr. Montolongo knows who he is fooling—
he has fooled everyone.
But his body is impatient: the fierce lily
of blood has opened more than once
in his chest, his brain,
and on each thigh.

There is only a little time left.
The thought of this makes him fret
when his wife leaves the house.
How can he die, his one heroic impulse,
when his wife comes and goes
so easily?

2

They say it will rain forever,
that February will keep
inventing itself.
His daughters chat in the kitchen,
packing tortillas with pork;
the young doctor stops by
to learn more about his death.

At the window, Mr. Montolongo
watches the brown puddles lapping

his doorstep, water mending
the grass and the street . . .

Death is all around us—
There: the leaves, the stars
of maple and corridors of bark
break off and float away.
If this is his chance,
his mast and plank,
he will hunch over
on the prow of a ship heading out.

In appreciation for life,
for its food and its daughters
whose hips swell like sullen clouds,
he will close his eyes
and let the lids settle
on their horizon of lashes.

If it rains, it will rain . . .
And if the sky clears

a man can always hold his open hand
up to the sunlight
and watch the bones stretch,
the white sail fill.

THE WAKE
FOR KEVIN KEEGAN

I bend over and lace up the shoes,
a half-moon of nails
sunk into each sole—the courage
to dance on your coffin.
These look like the feet of a nun
or an old man whose slack steps
drag him into their darkness.
But a cut must be precise,
a cross-key as swift
as the current off Kerry.
The waves fall, cracking
the rocks on the beach beneath them;
a small catch,
chafed on a loop of coarse yarn,
dances in the cold mournful wind.

*

All the Irish
who weren't dead
were drunk that night
in a small bar in San Francisco,
the last time breath entered
the leather ribs of the accordion
stretched on your chest.
Did you notice our fists
clenched at our sides,
our spines rigid
as we battered the floor

to keep up with your music?
Did you see the plow
edging a space for you
in the star-stung sky?
Your eyes closed on this:
the blur of feet, their stagger
in *the drunken man's step,*
in the wings of the blackbird
that has taken you there.

*

It was said
often in your family
that a rap on the door
would signal the death
of an uncle, a sister.
You'd wake to answer
and if no one was there,
you could be certain. Now,
the door is closed on you for good
and we could knock forever,
like Coleman or Keily
who challenged saints
for their share of a village.
Forced to dance for this vision,
our back feet fly on the wood.
But the earth wins you back
without trying.

Your friends,
slumped in the dull light
of the bar, finish their beers.

By dawn, the blackbird
has returned.

*

The body is burrowed in green;
the iron gates, beaded with fog,
are locked on the other country;
the stones, unable to carry
the tune of the hanging branch,
repeat themselves. The keening
moves only those left to hear it.

A white moon grazes the earthline,
completing the last furrow
where hard shoes trip through the dark
to find their way home.
They speak quickly, apologizing
to the animals and the ragged grass.
What is good for the right foot
will do for the left.
Like the pale stones,
each step repeats itself
in this world, and again
barely touching the next.

RUMOR

FOR LANCE AND MARGARET

One day, the old woman
decided they'd done it.
The world was crazy
and they'd get her too.
She loaded the gun
and went off to the garden
for a silver cabbage,
a fist of verbena
as usual. She bent over,
her head bobbing in the cool breeze,
first, "no," then slightly
consenting. She could be seen
from a distance and mistaken.
If they came from behind,
out of that piney bird's beak
or the greasy pipe
in the carport, there would be
no struggle. She'd tremble
and hand over the gun.
This was a perfect place
for planting. She saw her face
unfolding in the cabbage,
in the dull stars on the tin bucket
where the gun stood guard.
This worried her. She took
more than she wanted:
a carrot that would sweat;
an onion that would simmer beautifully,

shed each icy ring;
a winter pepper
that always fought back—
too many. Quickly,
she patted the dirt back over them.
From his porch, a neighbor
glanced at her—she nodded
the usual, "no . . . no,"
so he went on shaving.
But to the south
the house was empty,
the young couple missing;
the bare windows got darker
every day. The cabbage,
the silt on her fingertips
were forgotten. In silence
the piney bird nibbled
at a moldy leaf.

NAOMI'S HOUSE

An electric cable formed a triangle
with the sun and the alley
that ran behind the pool hall.
It was a sure silver needle
that could sew through hardpan,
hum like a busy woman over her work.
When I put my ear to its thin vibration
my mother pulled me away, pointing
to the danger sign—red Y's and O's,
like the fangs and eyes of an angry snake.
At midday, the steel was hot to the touch.

This was the power for Naomi's house;
her steam iron gasped
as she pressed the percale
and Philippine lace. No one
could match her work,
stiffen the shams where dreams nested,
or melt the snowy edges.
When she stopped to rest,
she lifted the hot face
like a mirror, tucking back
the stray hairs.
She knew everything about us
without leaving the house
more than twice a year.

On Sundays, the alley was empty
except for a few men who moved toward the Lotus Bar.

Naomi's house was locked and paintless,
its balcony slowly falling
like a long smile on its own shadow.
It looked as though it had been closed
for years—since her people hurried
into rooms beneath the street, preparing
to live in the darkness there.

The truth was that even there,
in the smokey chambers of earth,
the old men argued
about which way the Yangtze flowed:
one knowing he had never seen it,
the other with that look in his eyes,
the gleaming reflection of sun
and water on rock—simple proof
to his daughter who would grow
into the power and circles of light.

A SALE OF SMOKE

As the swamp cooler breathes
into the room the Chinese lamp
swings, bathing the girls' faces
with red half-moons. They wait
all night with sachets tucked
in their bras, skimming letters
or filing their toenails
into hearts. Through the grille
he points one out, one
unlike the others,
"I want that . . . she moves
like a snail." A half-moon
rises and follows him.

She can live in her own dark soil;
she can flip the sheets back
with one toe and lower her lids,
like yellowed shades,
against the heat. She can
give him what he wants.
For thirty cents, for thirty
beans . . . makes fifteen
for herself and fifteen
for mama, divided
like mice balls
and steamed to a mush. She can
live for another day.

Outside, in the city,
the day takes over. The vapor

lifts her lids again:
from the pool around the drinking post,
from the mush pots, and the clay jug
steeped with olive leaves
to get new men.
An old whore hikes her skirts,
leaping over the smoke twice,
and the one in bed feels
her pillow sink each time
the hag's feet hit the ground.
She tries to squeeze the life
back into her nipples,
"When I dry up I'll break a jug
over the last fucker's head."
Her fire has already started.

THE TRAVELER
FOR PETER

At the edge of the village,
battered stalks and then a field
of poppies. You drop your pack
to the ground, picking
the few that will last
until you find others.

Among the stalks,
an old farmer
whose plow has died.
Wearing these flowers
you remind him of his son
who let the fields
go to seed. Not everyone
will be quick to claim you:

you're a foreigner—
American—maybe a Messiah
whose gray hairs mingle
with the clouds,
and even slightly girlish
with the poppies swaying
behind one ear.

Later, you see men
like him again and again:
their shadows on dry grass,
their hats left on village walls,

and you want to call them
by name . . .
                But in the fields
the petals are stained glasses
filling quickly with sunlight
and dust; you tap the last dirt
from the roots and go on.

TERREMOTO:
ANTIGUA, 1976

It was the earth again
gathering the chips
of mica and flagstone.
Everything knelt down
a little too suddenly—
the biggest ears of corn,
the sow two feet from shade.
Cigarettes rolled
from the vendor's stand
across the park;
my friends from bed.

We had sworn
to leave her sometime,
but came back
with our collars straightened,
our hats socked into shape.
Now I watch my friend,
Tomás, turn toward the bar;
he is sick of being poor
and having those small wooden boxes
left at his doorstep
like gifts that will swallow
his children.

He says the way she edged
her rocky shoulders into his place
made her look like a man.

She lifts the mirror again,
letting him have it—
the dust that he is.

Tonight, we go by lamplight
to the stadium.
It is like the face
of the earth, puffy
with cotton mattresses,
wrinkled with arms and legs.
The green wash of grass
is still. But with the first tremor,
the bowl rocks and we can't sleep.
The lullaby begins—a song
she sings of how beautiful
she is, beautiful . . .

    and we always believe her.

THE FESTIVAL
OF FATIMA

At dusk, in the heart of summer,
the boats wait in the harbor
to be blessed, their planks scented
with the histories of fish,
nets falling from side to side
like the Virgin's veils.
A priest walks down the hill
to the beach beside men
carrying only bottles under their arms
for the one storm they look forward to.
When the priest lifts his arms
the hem of his white skirt
floats out over the brine,
away from Nazaré,
like a giant sail.

The stars come out:
women imitate the night, men
the water and fish, growing fins
to find their way home.
In the bars, every stool is taken,
every eye dark and hardened
as the first flecks of rot on a mackerel.
Old Fatima—voluptuous grandmother
who saves men by lying full weight
on the waters she loves.
Saint of the rolling masses,
of pausing and falling,

Mother of the sand
and men who prefer the moist hips
of a big woman. They can't get
your scent off their hands.

A few will leave the bars
and the drink that makes them
talk to you and go sit on the beach,
waiting for your vision.
It could take all night,
until the women leave church
and the buses depart for the smaller villages,
until one stops to point out
over there—the new world, uncrossed,
eating its blessing of sunlight.

 THREE

STORY

Weighted with snow,
the hemlock branches
hang to the ground.
To keep from dreaming
the mare drags her tail
through the swollen needles
and powders the air,
then backs up
butting her hooves
until the chips of ice
fall away.

At dark, old winter-woman
speaks into the mare's ear,
gives her a slice of moon
that looks like a carrot,
and leads her gently
over the mountain—
they never come back.

We ask the cold for directions,
but it is silent.
The screech of the road salter
carries for miles—
the deer flinch,
the river remembers
her husband who drank
all summer.

We climb the mountain,
following the tracks
of an animal threaded
through those of a snowmobile.

Winter,
infiltrator of soft linings,
perfect tooth of stone,
thief of horses
and children . . .
When we call, our voices
turn and come meekly
back to us.

2

Rain washes one county
into the next,
mud over bones
and matted branches of hemlock.
No trace of the familiar,
there is no chance
of finding something
that was lost the month before.

The curves in the trail
now lead to a pool
of lost ice, the rocks
sleep together,
their mouths hanging open,
the smooth hindquarters
of the mountain are mulched
with needles and ground fern.

But we are young enough
to watch the old woman
bury her mask
and make her getaway:

she is the screech owl
that falls to the road,
like a rock,
frightening the deer,
the skull of the mare
that flapped off in the breeze.

AT DAWN

1

Magnolia scepters,
amulets of moths,
the sheen of snail balm
on new limbs.
A woman fluffs pillows
until they look like her eyes,
a man left wiping the bar
barely sees himself
in the slur of bottles,
a child grips the crib bars
singing to the gold thread
at the edge of the shade.

In the darkened room
she lifts the child to her;
the sunlight knits itself
into a sweater that they can wear
over their shoulders
through the day.

2

Late at night,
my mother would kiss me
when she thought I was asleep,
watching the bulb of dreams
break open. Now,
I crawl out

through the cave of blankets,
bringing what I am
with me: gold tooth,
eyes like two milky planets,
anything that will
catch the light.

3

Steal an upturned leaf
and it crumbles,
stare down a blackbird
and it bursts into flames.
The only way to own light
is by accident.

When it is overhead
the children kneel at the gutter,
dipping for worms
until their nails
flicker like candles.
Or they run down the sidewalk,
putting their hands into pockets
where the pale sky sleeps
a few more hours.

THE TREES BEGAN TO SPEAK

The trees began to speak and this frightened her,
deep chanting fir
using the lips of those she knew.
When the sky darkened and the air cooled
the voices became clearer.
There were twice as many stars
as ever before. In her heart,
a valley where there were no trees
and the sky kept to itself.

She had always been known
for peeking into the lives of others,
for throwing the windows open
to let the million fearsome insects
float off in the breeze.
She was also known for dancing in strong winds
that showed her real strength.

If you've seen a skirt of dust
whirl down from the Sierra
and heard the rag jangled out
on the keyboard of scrub and pine
you're probably a distant relative.

She will visit you soon.

2

By morning

the mountains were covered with people.
The sunlight made it clear who they were—
those lugging pails of water uphill,
children scampering over the beds of needles
as though there were no mountains.

Across the lake
men snoozed under blankets of hair
and swamp grass; three women
entered the water in perfect harmony.
She couldn't hear what they were saying,
but could see their lips move
and feel the ringing in her bones.

3

Oarlock screwed into splintered wood,
paddle nudging the sandy shoal,
the boat came toward her . . .

She dressed in the shadows of redwoods,
she stirred the ashes with dust and lake water,
counting the carbonous specimens,
the last moments of solitude
before it arrived.

It mattered less that the boat was empty
than where it would take her.

4

So what if trees spoke?
She had listened too carefully.

It was good that they had their secret language.
They shouldn't remind you of a friend
giving advice, or your old aunt
warning you to stay away from a certain man.
They shouldn't make you think
of ancestors pacing the earth,
drawling the stories you heard as a child.
They shouldn't make you think of yourself.

The boat was built from the wood
of trees brought closer to earth
by the wind, the wind braiding
the light in the branches,
in the wings of a wading bird
who had the world to himself.

This was the last time she would see
her body rise like a trunk
through the seasons of water
and remember everything
she had ever learned.

"A MAGIC THING"
ROUZAT, 1904

Everything is moving:
the river through the field
of wild crocus, children
pitching stones into the shallow water.
In a café on the far side,
on the banks carved out by currents,
she is dancing with the man
who took these pictures.
As they sway, she keeps her eyes
on the row of poplars,
small mirrors turning
toward sunlight. She thinks:

They are all there—
in the sky, in the river
tugging at the ropes of grass,
in the wine she drinks—

and that the dancing will go on
forever.

*

I smooth the pages
on her half of the century,
a life as black and white
as the crows rising from the poplars
or certain thoughts
that weren't encouraged.

And when she smiles,
the full red lips burn
through the gray rings of paper.
The things that make us smile
have changed. Perhaps

if there hadn't been the wars,
the crocus stripped by dark
between her childhood and mine . . .
Or if the man hiding
under the black felt hood
had fallen off his stool!

Is this a trick?
The flash of light that leaves
its crystals on our shoulders,
the wind trembling
in the broken reeds, afraid
of being saved without a reason.

MEDITATION

I could sit in this hot bath for hours
both ends disappearing at once
old skin sloughed and lacy
as bits of lichen
until only my navel
a stone cast
leaves rings on the surface
and the water closes over it.

I am the reed
you peeled back and snapped
off your bare shoulder
a slow spear
that landed ever so lightly
on the glassy lake
and stayed afloat.

My arms
even my chin
are weightless . . .

and I could almost go under
without a breath—
the water like a mother
with her gloves and small parcel
saying *I brought you here*
and I can take you back.

TONSILS

Two seahorses smiled at me
from a glass of water on the nightstand,
two wishbones of the speech

I wished for.
There were two pink and fibrous roots
picked from a forest

or were they my mother's fingers
pressed twice their size
as she held the glass for me to drink?

I remember it perfectly
though the hospital danced in fog
at 4 A.M.

I was dressed in the blues
of an absent child, to be undressed
by those in gray

calling me back to sleep.
And I swam back, like the small horses,
through the sheets of foam

and water with land on all sides.
The blade trimmed,
mahogany walled and drifted,
glass held water.

2

The hospital is gone,
the rows of small windows sucked out
and scattered over a foundation

that leads back to earth.
Nearly everyone is missing something.
But few remember the colors

or the silence that pushes us away
from its world.
This is a memory of beginnings,

of creatures more exotic
than redworms or stunned flies.
It is to be spoken without swallowing:

a memory painless
as a hen's bone broken for a second time
on a new wish, as a root

lifted gently from the mud,
or clear water
without a name for it.

THE FEAR OF ANGELS

Neither was the man created for the woman;
but the woman for the man.
For this cause ought the woman to have power
on *her* head because of the angels.

—I Corinthians 11:9,10

It is amazing that I've never mentioned my hair.
But then, there is so little of it
surviving independently,
like a hermit with his diet of grain.

It hasn't changed at all
since I came out of my mother,
the fringe of my imagination
still caught in the womb,
the tail of an escaping animal.

Thin, fine . . .
I could be any age.
It takes its shape from the wind,
its texture from the nest.
It is only as good as the few
golden strands the sun gives
which would slip through your fingers.

There are women who cover their heads
out of the fear of angels—

they have good reason:
a crown of thick tendrils,
a forest of wisps
that would tempt any man.
Their scarves only make it worse.

But the one who thinks
he can lose his fingers in my hair
can have his way.
It won't take long for him to learn the truth.
Until then, I can enjoy
the sound of his wings
beating in my ears.

THE BAT

1

In autumn,
the bats steamed in their fur
like rotten eggs
buried under each shingle.
We looked up—
the ladder shook
as the man pried their fists
loose with a crowbar.
In one burst,
they shot dead-eyed
into the thicket.

2

Bats never go away;
they settle nearby
on the darkest limbs
where they grow
and get uglier.
In a year's time
they wriggle back
into the beams and nests
of barnstraw, whispering.
The heifers wear out
their heels in the paddock;
people blow softly
into the currents of sleep,

their hands
open at their sides.

3

Before dawn,
I ease into dreams,
a quilt stretched
over my knees. The little ones
crawl out, fanning
themselves: *pouch-winged*,
graceful *pallid*, I am ready.
Leaf-nosed can't see
me coming and waits
on the last rib
for a slow moth. I steal
his edge on darkness.

4

Bluejay rams a cherry tree,
hummingbird rests its head
on the bar, asks for another,
the phoebe gives away
her drab color, the wretched crow
gives up and begs for a field mouse
who can't understand.

The answer is the bat
who finds life easy
to swallow. He drops here

like a hankie, but leaves
his song in the other world—
he too is a failure. Try again.

5

So you took
two clipped steps
toward the window, the curtain
swelled. He was asleep
and with each gust spread
like a burn over the white lace.
You opened a book
and closed it around his body,
tilting the binding
until he fell two floors down
to the bed of dahlias
where the sun began
and the wind, in one word,
offered itself to the earth.

NIGHTFALL ON PACHECO

1

Cattle perch on the boulders above the road,
watching trucks pass in the twilight.
Oak and sycamore gather on the river bottom,
like widows holding the darkness. And there,

the lizard traffics on the long ribbon
of sand, a linen cloth
laid out under the new moon.

His trail angles off behind him
through the night—
a curve, a letter, a fiery history.
Our headlights catch the animals

staring back, asking us
what becomes of them.

2

We have driven this road so many times
it leaves little to talk about;
you know so well its shaded curves and gorges.

But I can only remember another man
who followed the rough striations
of these hills, lumbering too long
on the wrong side of the line
braided loosely down the shoulder.

In the end, the sun sucked the autumn fields
down to the last thistle and tongue's share
of dust. It took the small mirror
between its fingers, the strand of hair,
the piece of cloth.

It slipped each silver spoke under its lips,
like new teeth,
and then swallowed itself.
I trembled in the shadows for weeks.

3

The nightfall is a final breath,
a mixture of blue gasses
that inherits our motion.

Only the lizard can see it this way,
through eyes that run close to the ground:

sprawled out over the mountains,
the shadow dug by the setting sun,
the weak spot in the widow's circle
where he will break through.

He pauses
and swallows the pulse in his rubbery neck.

He must live in this place,
only partially disguised,
for as long as he can.

CROWS

A perfect place for a congregation of crows.
High up on the bough of a new fir
rigid under all that weight,
a dead man's arm.
They have a lot to say
to the heavens and each other,
each with the mutter of someone below.
Beneath them, tarred roofs and empty roads,
the open palm of a cemetery:
a woman kneels and enters
the small square of flowers.
Sycamores line the streets
in the older section where the light
is a voice filtering down through the leaves.
My father has told me about men
who spray the open branches with BBs,
watching the torn swatches of night
cross the sun. They wake up the next day
to find themselves missing,
their speech gone. You tell me
not to believe my father.
We're having a nice walk,
but you want to cross the shadow
of that fir and let the darkness
fly with a chunk of gravel;
the crows, skilled mechanics,
slip in and out of their greasy suits.
But I warn you:

a crow can outsmart a man,
stealing his voice, shouting
into the long funnel of God's ear.

IN THE WIND

The harpy eagle cracks a strange smile
as she dives to the chunks of meat
scattered on the floor of the aviary.
She has no memory of light
falling through the cow's eyes
or water foaming at its flanks.
Flight is the quickest way
of getting what she wants.
The warmth of animals makes her
shudder, the vast wings
fold earthbound.
Mistaken for a large rock,
she makes a resting place
for sparrows who slip through the wires.

Children, barely able to tell the difference
between themselves and birds,
shake the fence, their laughter
stirring the feathers.
But I jump back when she lands
a few feet from us into the shadow
of an empty tree. They say
the wind is the last song of her enemy.

*

This morning the sky had cleared
and the sun had climbed the steps
to our house. There,
our cat had left another bird—

one so young it never saw
what happened. Pale,
featherless,
only a faint pulse
as it waded back into the river
to learn its future
and wash its broken wings.
I wrapped it in a rag
and took it into the day
as though the sun would change
its mind, as though the web
of stems and leaves would open
like a trapdoor
for those who should survive.

*

When some of us die
we ask for air,
more air, like birds too small
to stay adrift. But,
like the harpy, you begged
for water and nourishment.
The birds you knew
cruised the islands of the Pacific
for days on nothing
but the crust of salt in their beaks.
And when they said
you looked like a bird
because you were dying
you made a sound that summoned
the wind. You entered
the gentle currents of your name,

Serafin, and with all three wings
touched the horizon
and disappeared.

*

The sycamores shiver;
the bark snaps in the chill air.
These are the signs I look for.

Others are peck marks
on the cat's own birdlike skull,
feathers hinged to fur,
bones that fall from the highest branches.
When you give my bones to the earth
the grass will grow back quickly;
I will never write about birds again.
And if the harpy tries to sing
in the wind, cover your ears
and study the lips of those around you.

It is a song that rips the sky,
it has nothing to do with love.

SILKS

I The Silk Maker

He lives in the same house with the worms,
and his fingers are the first to touch their heavens.

In the morning, the sun whitens the glass
and the suited shadows step out on the street
to do business; he leaves his bed
and quietly crosses the room to the box,
then to the stove,
setting a pan of water over the blue flame.
Arrows of light enter, rumple the blankets,
ignite his fingers. He dips the cocoons

into the layers of steam and water,
until they float to the surface
and are skimmed off,
as one man would strop the foam from his beer
or another clears the skies
on an autumn day. The only hint of a storm:

a thimble of broken leaves,
the thread of dust
winding, like an invisible path, to the gates
where God is a yellow moth

that flutters the eyelids open
and the day begins again.

II

Like silk, I am spun on two families—
the tree and the cloud,
the branch respecting the sky that flees
from itself.

It was after the war and my father was home,
my uncles, cousins—all men
flew back to their families,
except for my grandfathers
who heard the rumbling from their graves.
Times were good and everyone had their silks:

my aunts, black market stockings
that they wore in the cities,
my father his flier's maps of Formosa
and the Philippines folded in the dresser,
and the ash trees their veils of rust-colored leaves.

In September, on the day of my birth,
the translucent fibers filled the air,
sticking to cars, windows, fences and tree trunks.

Blown over on his back, a caterpillar
begged the wind to help him look for his shoes.

III

I am now the person you know,
you can see who I am.

I step out of the bath and walk to the bedroom;
I will not change again without warning.

There,
on the bed, are my pajamas,
woven and stitched in Taiwan.
A lotus for each breast and one
for each crazy bone.

An old woman hung them over a branch
and lowered it into the blue river;
a man with one leg eased the elastic
into the waistband; a new housewife
fastened the frog at the neck
and kissed it when no one was looking,
then packed them into a box marked *America*.
I wear this history, this secondhand clothing,
and still I am the person you know.

I blot the moisture off my back,
unpin my hair, and put them on:

this is the ascot, the tiny glove, the chemise;
this is the sleeping gown of the worm.
How lucky I am!
What dreams I will have.

But I will not change again without warning.

IV Ailanthus

It has learned the contours of America well:
the arc of its branches, the fatness of stones
and flexibility of leaves
where it curls.
It has a sixth sense for progress
and readies itself for a new contribution.

Ailanthus stops eating,
throws up what's left of its name
from the infinite caves of intestines,
and chooses its twig
as a woman would pick a man
for his stability and uprightness.
It returns its earthly possessions
to the *tree of heaven*,
and wades into the shallow pond
of its own mucus, quivering
like a wick, the flame
waxed over.

A true Christian,
this creature covers its head first
with a fine veil, leaving a space
through which it will see the sky again
one day, after the Cross has passed over
and the last shadow is gone from the earth.

We call this *a worm*
as it coils into the final,

veinous skin of its own life
and makes fools of us all.

V

Eggshell, sperm case,
bed sheet and burrow lining,
hinges, trapdoors,
noose or dragline,
the gossamer takes to air
at the whim of a current—
life is not easy.

Men with money on their minds
brought ailanthus to this country,
like rum or the blacks,
but my mother brought me.
Don't tell me how fortunate I am,
how rich. Like the others

I go out, set up my table at the corner,
and open my pockets
before the sun has left the market.
I flatter,
contrive purposes, imagine colors
no one would wear,
and hawk these goods.

Calling, *the essence of snow,*
cloud morsel, a skin
so much finer than your own,
I speak magic, but breathe the dust.

It clouds the air
as I tip the box o
the last fragment
wiping the wood

Ailanthus, no on
the branch leadin
would be beautifɪ
We take our silks
and musty odor,
from its molded l

ABOUT THE AUTHOR

Roberta Spear was born in 1948 in Hanford, California, where she also grew up. She received her B.A. and M.A. from California State University at Fresno, and was the 1979 winner of the James D. Phelan Award. Her poems have appeared in many magazines, among them The New Yorker, Antaeus, Field, The Nation, and Ironwood. Silks is her first collection of poetry. She currently lives in Winston-Salem, North Carolina, with her husband.

IV Ailanthus

It has learned the contours of America well:
the arc of its branches, the fatness of stones
and flexibility of leaves
where it curls.
It has a sixth sense for progress
and readies itself for a new contribution.

Ailanthus stops eating,
throws up what's left of its name
from the infinite caves of intestines,
and chooses its twig
as a woman would pick a man
for his stability and uprightness.
It returns its earthly possessions
to the *tree of heaven*,
and wades into the shallow pond
of its own mucus, quivering
like a wick, the flame
waxed over.

A true Christian,
this creature covers its head first
with a fine veil, leaving a space
through which it will see the sky again
one day, after the Cross has passed over
and the last shadow is gone from the earth.

We call this *a worm*
as it coils into the final,

veinous skin of its own life
and makes fools of us all.

V

Eggshell, sperm case,
bed sheet and burrow lining,
hinges, trapdoors,
noose or dragline,
the gossamer takes to air
at the whim of a current—
life is not easy.

Men with money on their minds
brought ailanthus to this country,
like rum or the blacks,
but my mother brought me.
Don't tell me how fortunate I am,
how rich. Like the others

I go out, set up my table at the corner,
and open my pockets
before the sun has left the market.
I flatter,
contrive purposes, imagine colors
no one would wear,
and hawk these goods.

Calling, *the essence of snow,*
cloud morsel, a skin
so much finer than your own,
I speak magic, but breathe the dust.

It clouds the air
as I tip the box over, tapping
the last fragments, the wings and scales,
wiping the wood for a new day.

Ailanthus, no one said
the branch leading to heaven
would be beautiful.
We take our silks from its thorns
and musty odor,
from its molded leaves.

ABOUT THE AUTHOR

Roberta Spear was born in 1948 in Hanford, California, where she also grew up. She received her B.A. and M.A. from California State University at Fresno, and was the 1979 winner of the James D. Phelan Award. Her poems have appeared in many magazines, among them The New Yorker, Antaeus, Field, The Nation, and Ironwood. Silks is her first collection of poetry. She currently lives in Winston-Salem, North Carolina, with her husband.